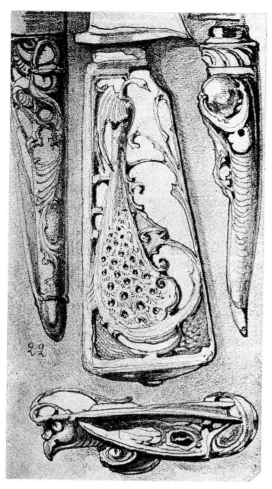

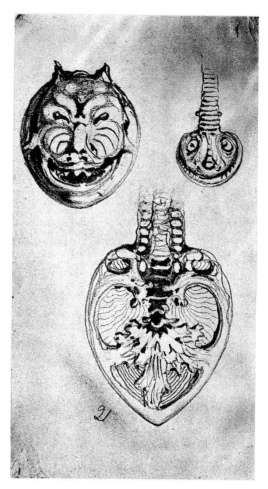

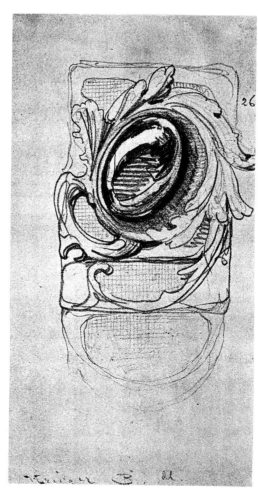

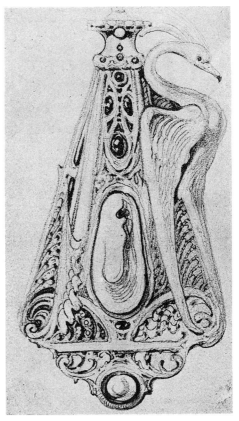

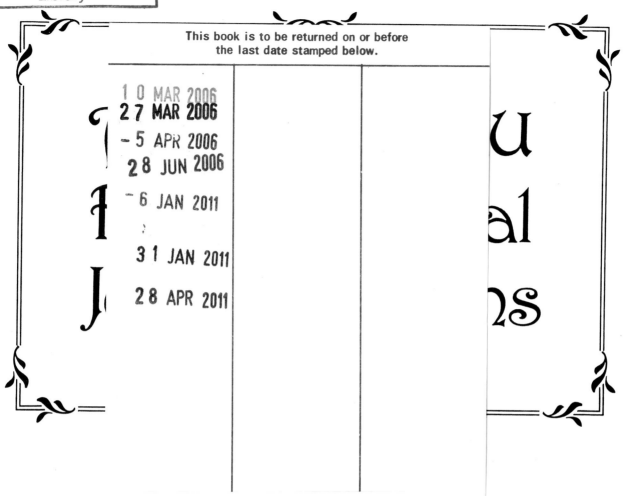

DOVER PUBLICATIONS, INC.
Mineola, New York

PUBLISHER'S NOTE

Between 1890 and 1910 the style known as Art Nouveau held sway in European and American decorative arts, and influenced, to a lesser degree, architecture. A reaction to the acute historicizing that had dominated most of the nineteenth century, it featured asymmetry and swirling forms derived from nature. If Art Nouveau had any precedent, it is to be found in the rocaille of the Louis XV period.

The Art Nouveau style lent itself especially well to jewelry, the works created by such masters as Alphonse Mucha and Louis Comfort Tiffany being among the best known. There was, however, a wealth of lesser-known artists-craftsmen, whose work was of the highest quality. Chief among their number is Béla-Gyula Krieger (b. 1861), here represented by illustrations from a rare portfolio of original designs that are as beautiful as they are bizarre. Hungarian-born, he spent most of his career in Paris. A talented *animalier* (see pp. 50–51) with an ironclad technique, Krieger also possessed an extremely vivid imagination. The studies on pp. 52–53, for example, bring to mind the nightmare world of Hieronymous Bosch.

Krieger was able to bring his imagination to bear on a wide variety of objects—both practical and purely decorative. These pages abound with designs for flatware, pendants, buckles, combs, even sword hilts.

Copyright

Copyright © 1997 by Dover Publications, Inc.
All rights reserved under Pan American and International Copyright Conventions.

Published in Canada by General Publishing Company, Ltd., 30 Lesmill Road, Don Mills, Toronto, Ontario.

Published in the United Kingdom by Constable and Company, Ltd., 3 The Lanchesters, 162–164 Fulham Palace Road, London W6 9ER.

Bibliographical Note

Art Nouveau Fantasy Animal Jewelry Designs, first published by Dover Publications, Inc., in 1997, is a republication of illustrations originally published by Armand Guérinet, Librairie d'Art décoratif, Paris, in *La Chimère & l'Animal et leur Application Ornementale à l'art du Bijou,* n. d. A new Publisher's Note has been written specially for the Dover edition.

DOVER *Pictorial Archive* SERIES

Library of Congress Cataloging-in-Publication Data

Krieger, Béla-Gyula, b. 1861
[Chimère & l'animal et leur application ornementale à l'art du bijou. English]
Art nouveau fantasy animal jewelry designs / B. Krieger.
p.   cm. — (Dover pictorial archive series)
Translation of: La chimère & l'animal e leur application ornementale à l'art du bijou.
Paris : A. Guérinet, Librairie d'art décoratif, [n.d.].
ISBN 0-486-29631-8 (pbk.)
1. Krieger, Béla-Gyula, b. 1861—Themes, motives. 2. Decoration and ornament—France—Art nouveau. 3. Animals, Mythical, in art. 4. Jewelry—France—Design. I. Title. II. Series.
NK7398.K75A4   1997
739.27'092—dc21
97-867
CIP

Manufactured in the United States of America
Dover Publications, Inc., 31 East 2nd Street, Mineola, N.Y. 11501

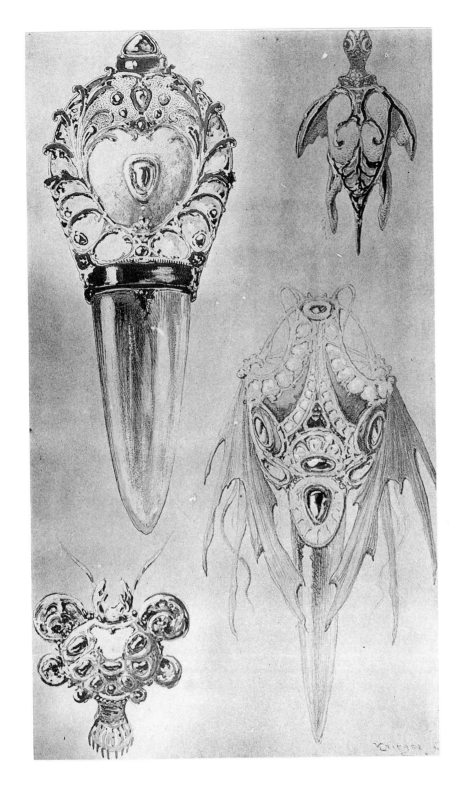

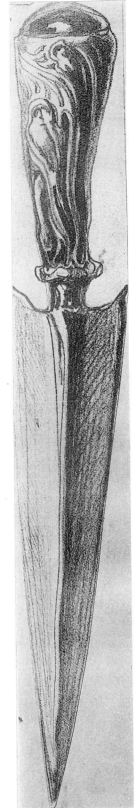

4

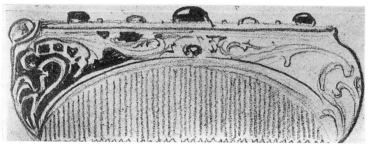

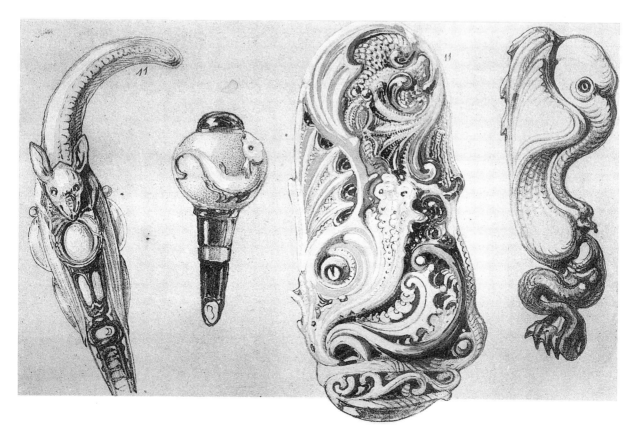

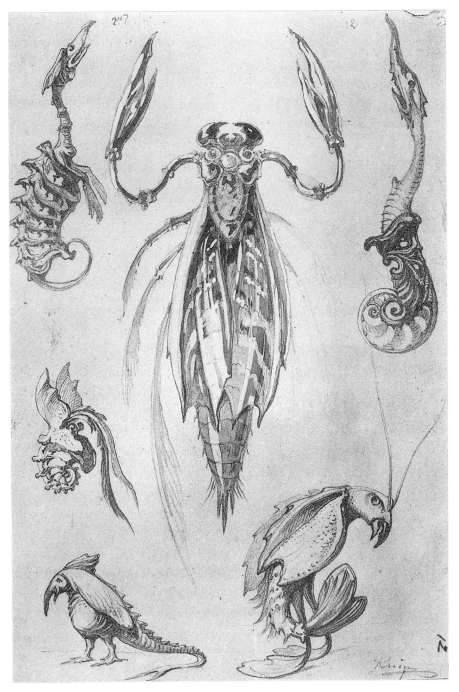

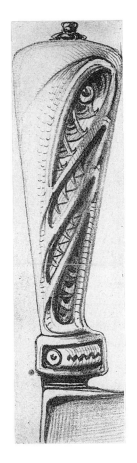

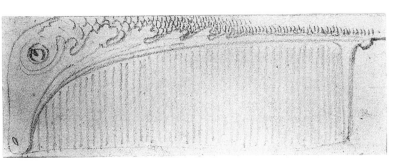

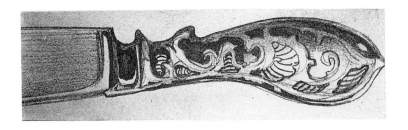

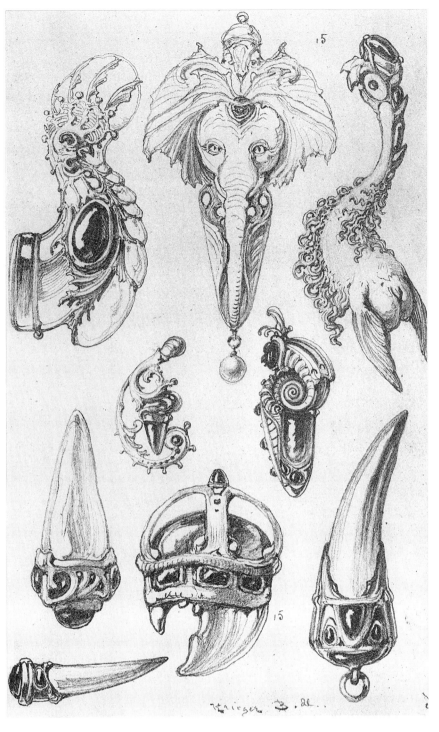

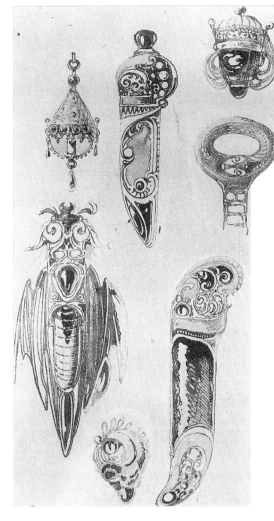

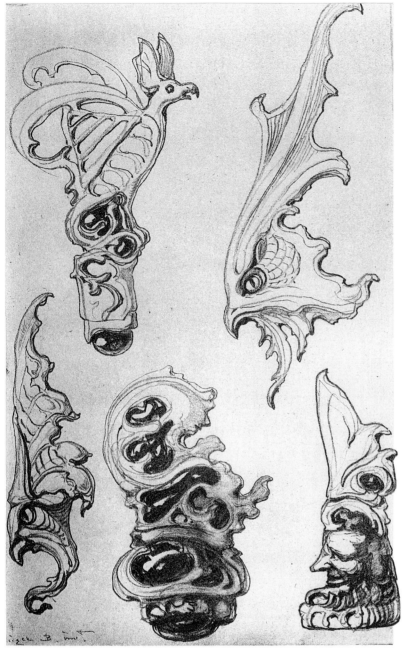

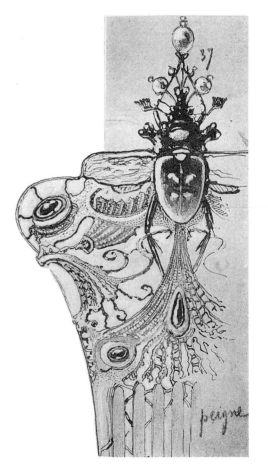

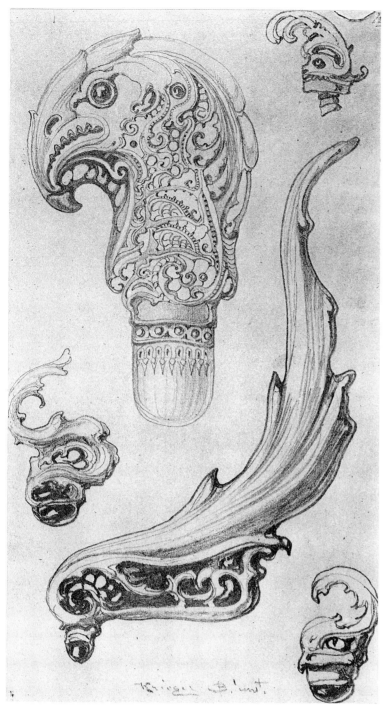

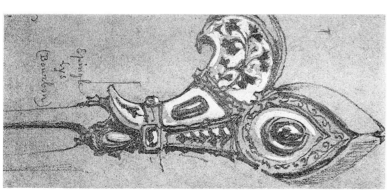

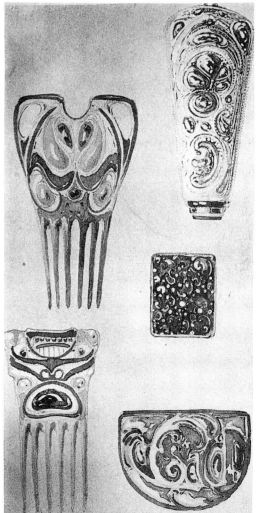

9

10

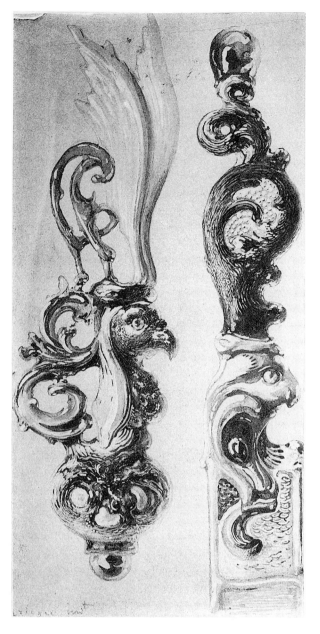

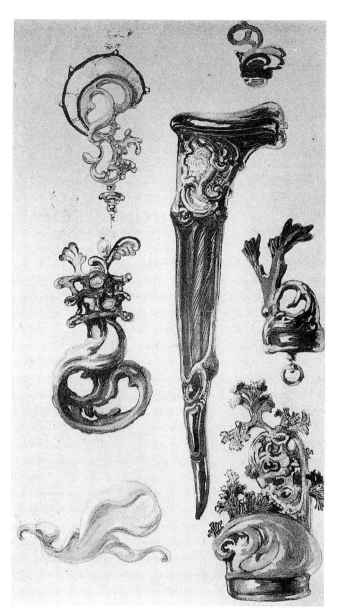

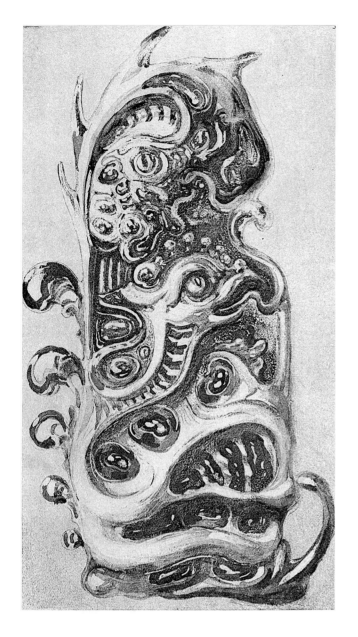

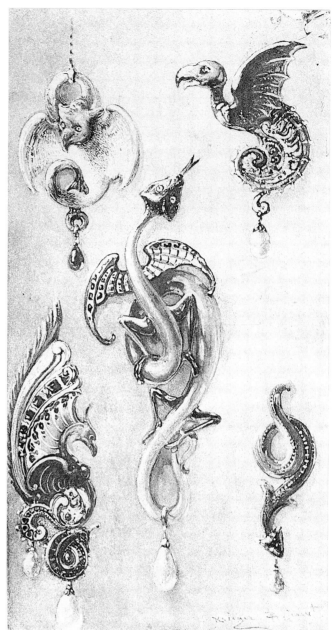

13

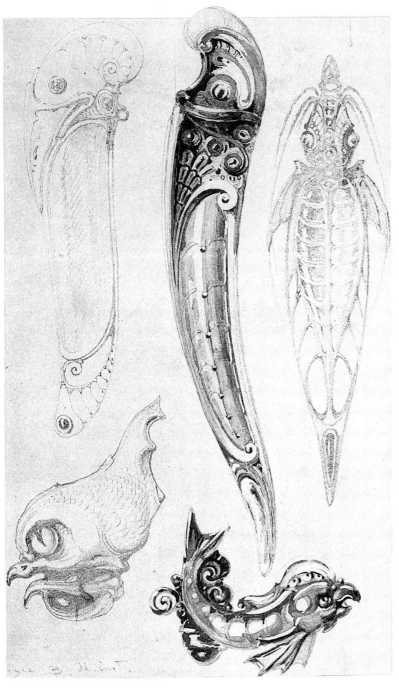

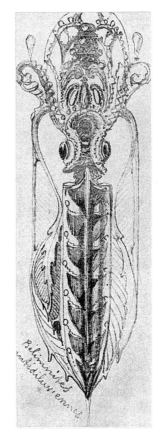

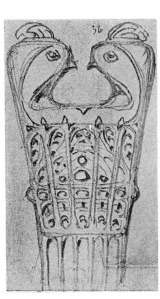

14

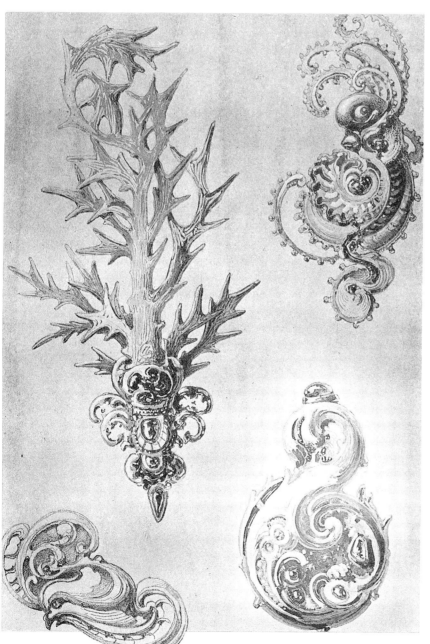

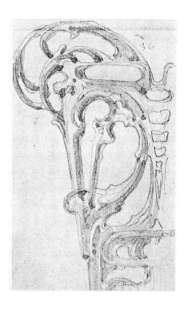

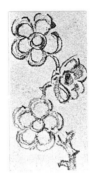

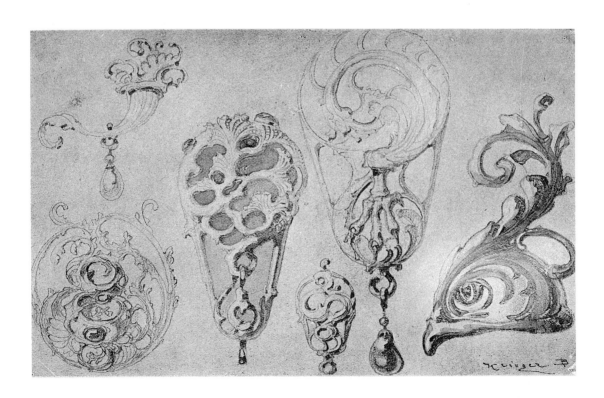

16

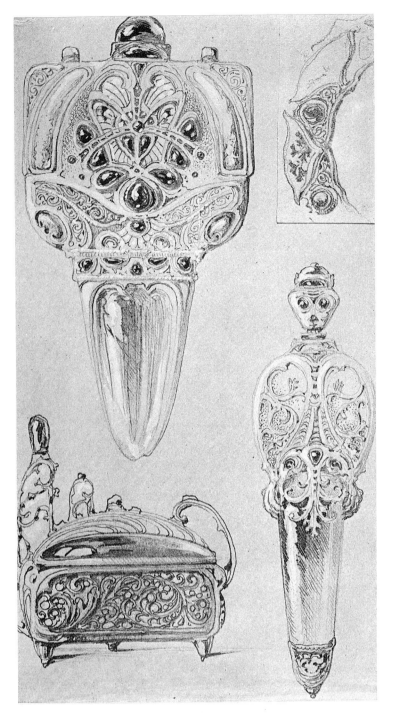

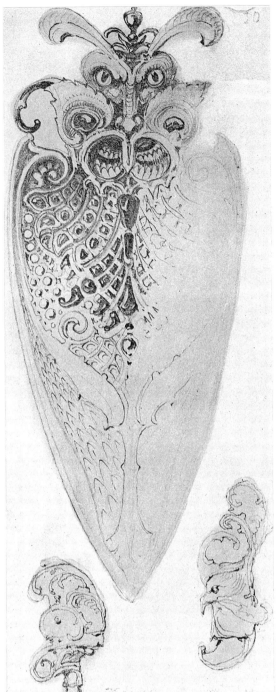

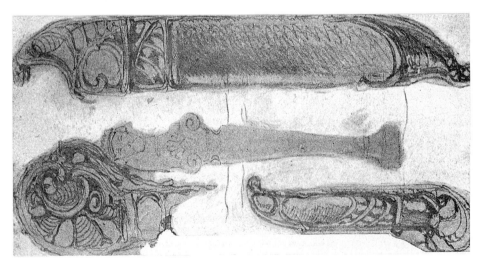

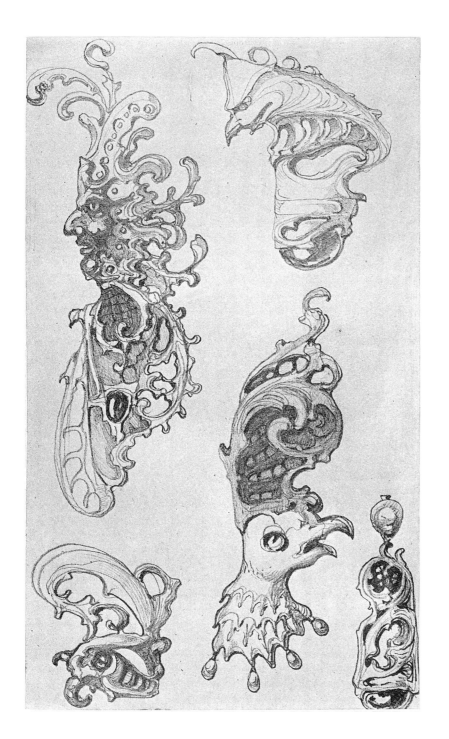

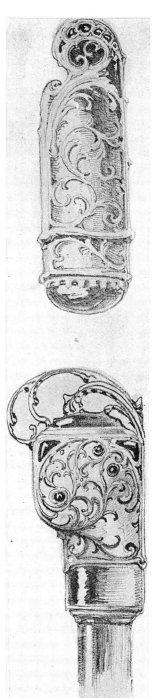

19

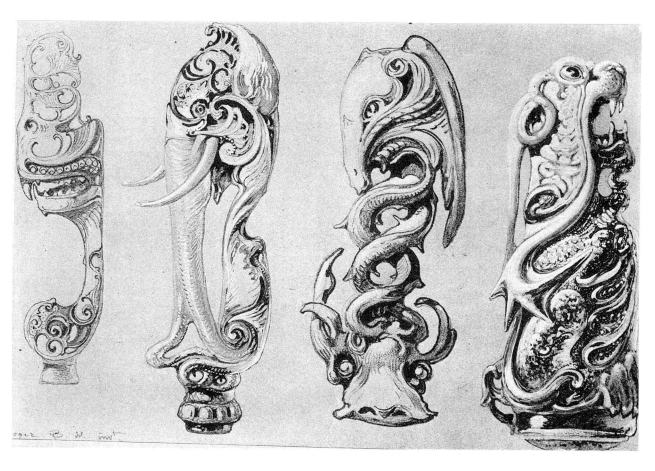

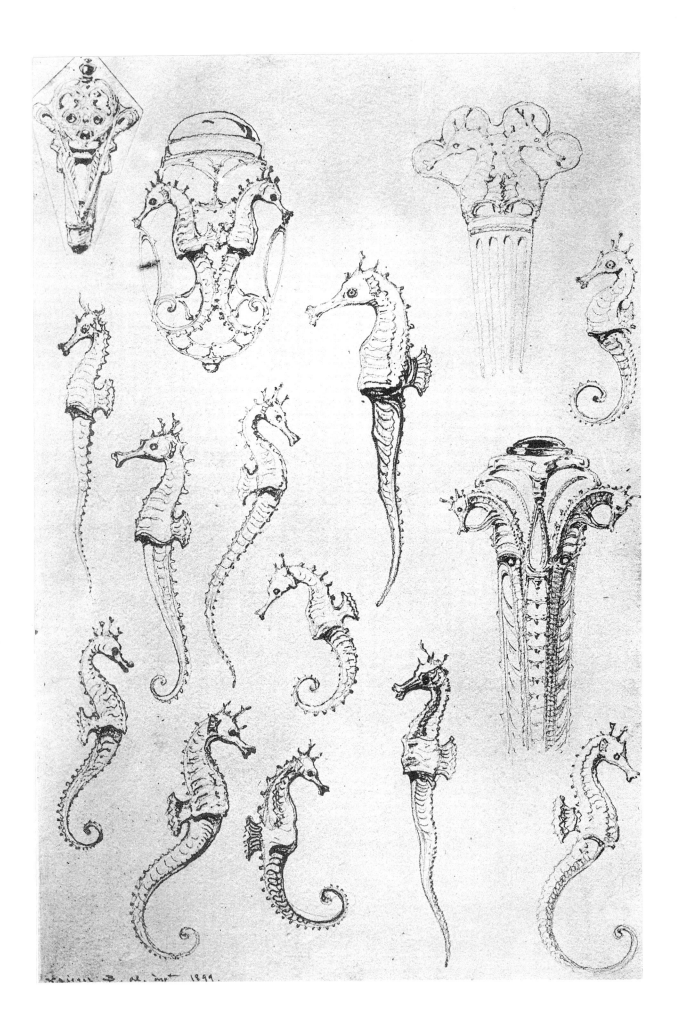

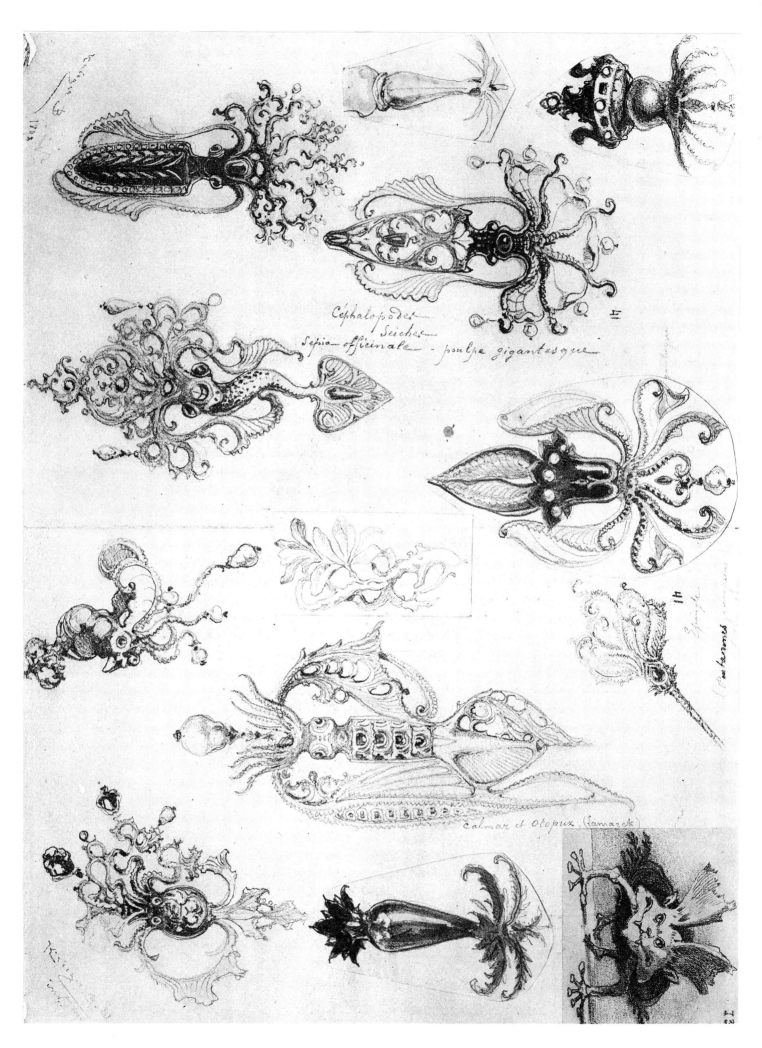

Céphalopödes
Seiches
Sepia officinale - poulpe gigantesque

Calmar et Otopux (Lamarck)

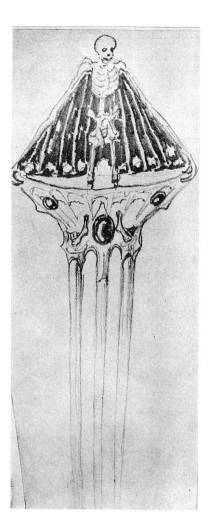

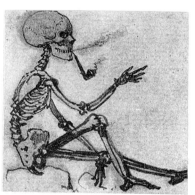

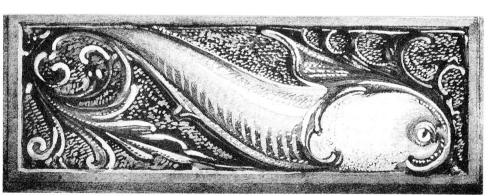

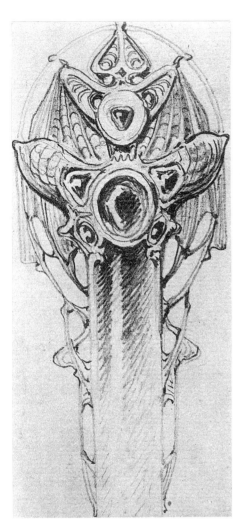

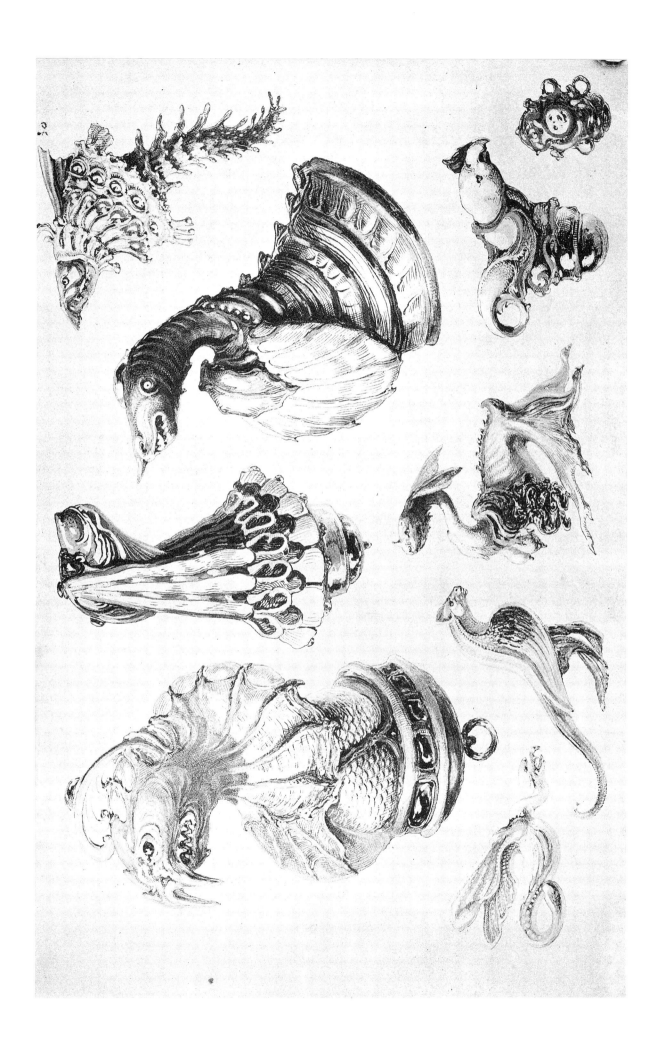

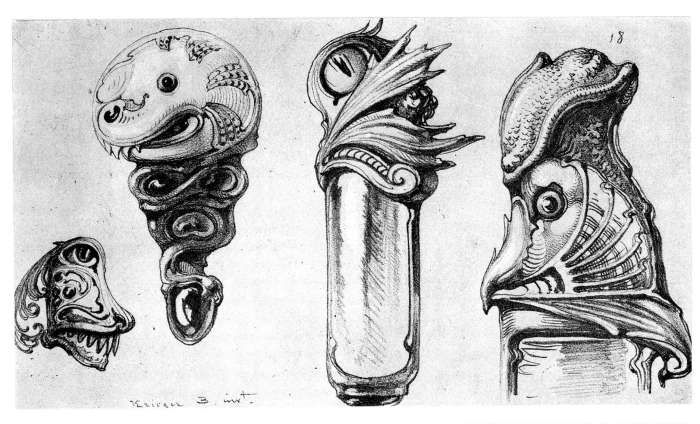

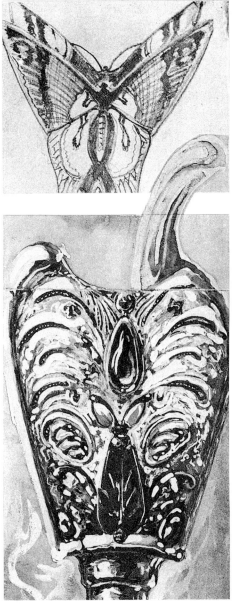

28

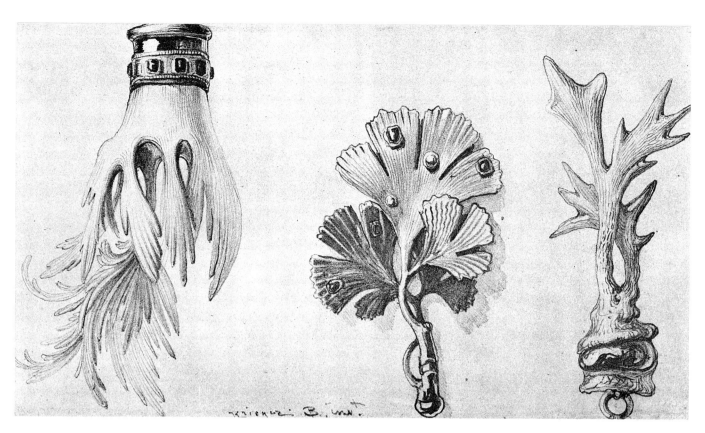

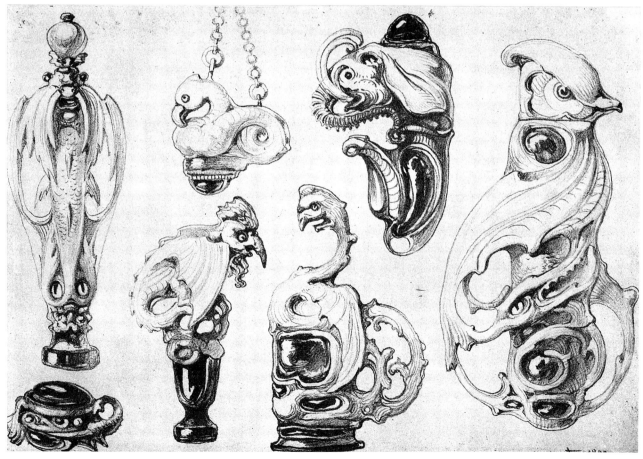

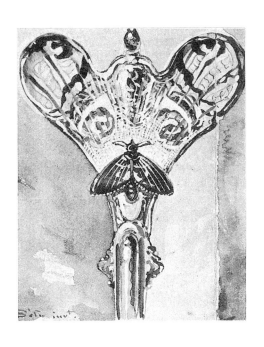

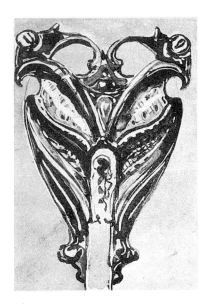

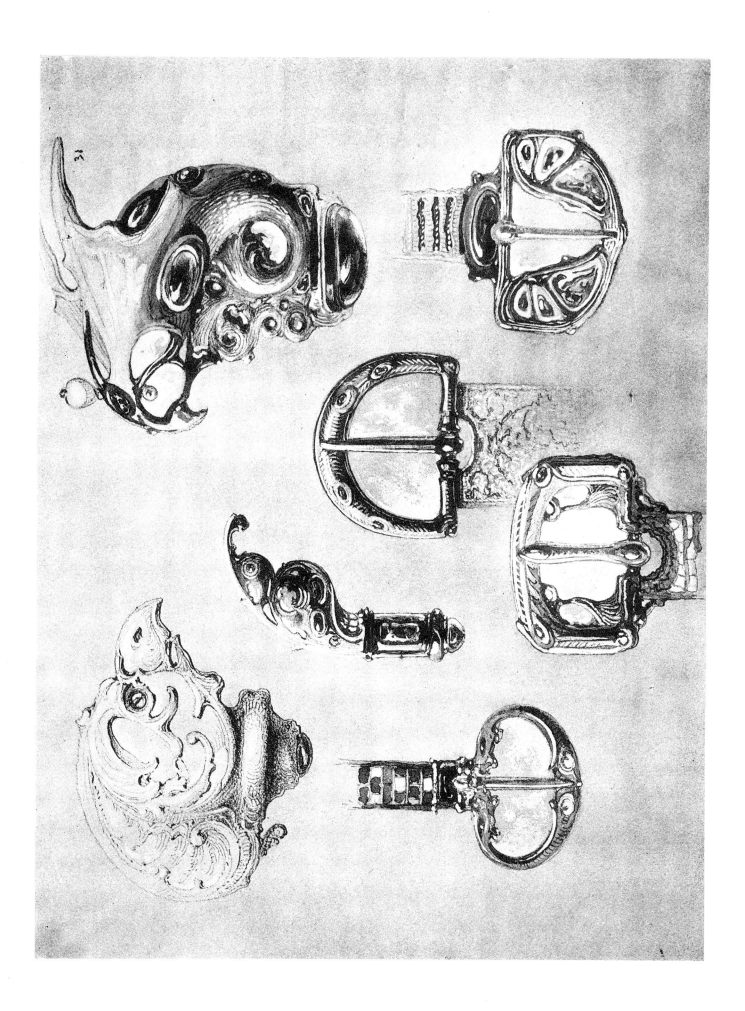

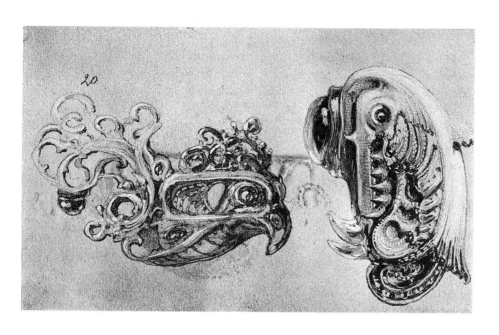

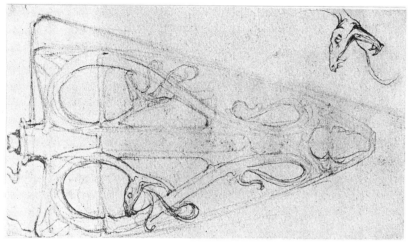

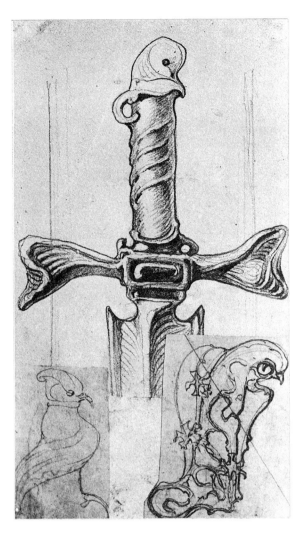

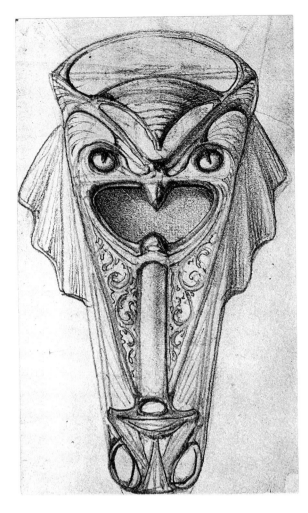

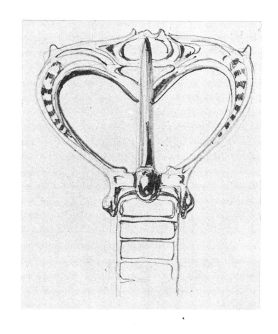

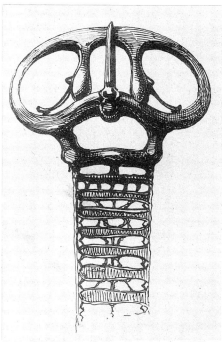

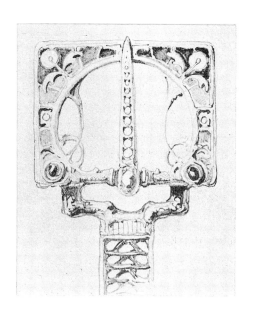

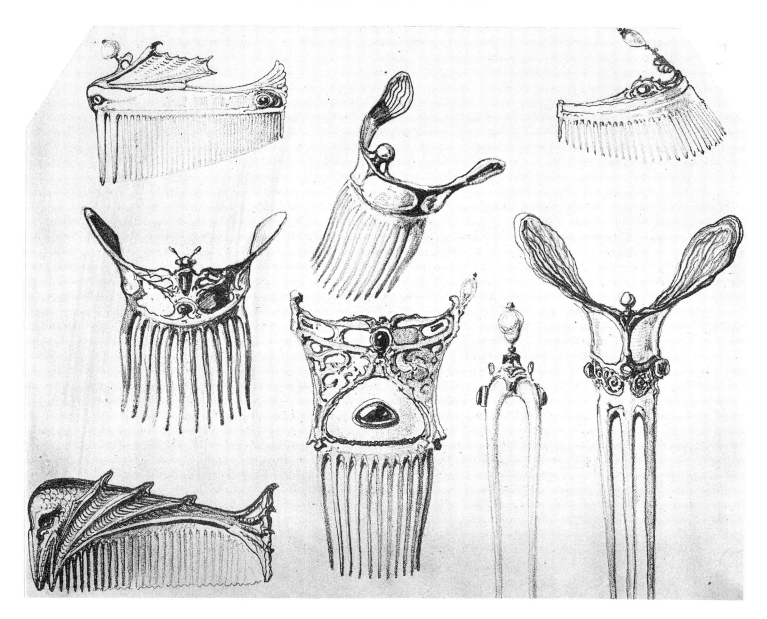

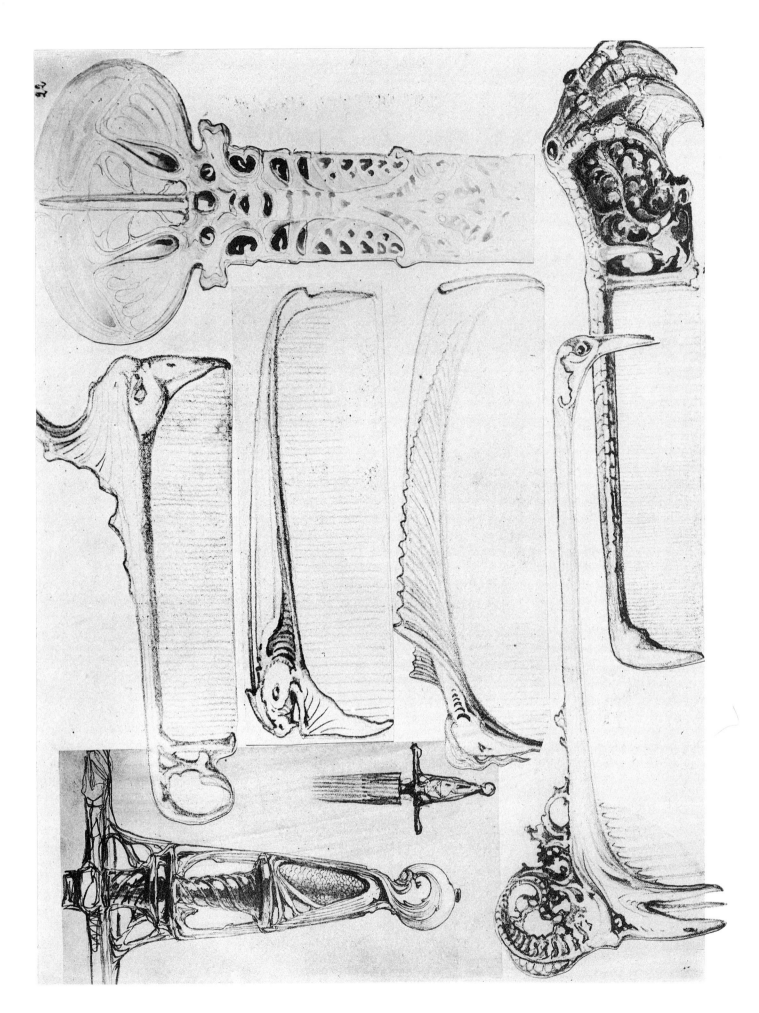

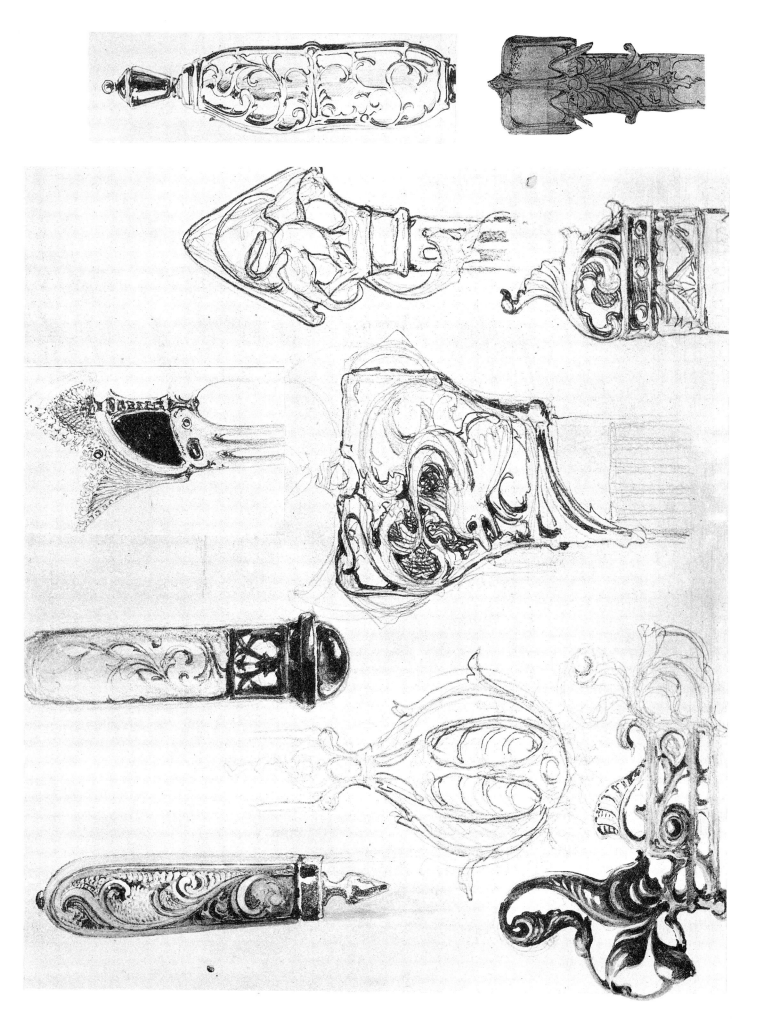

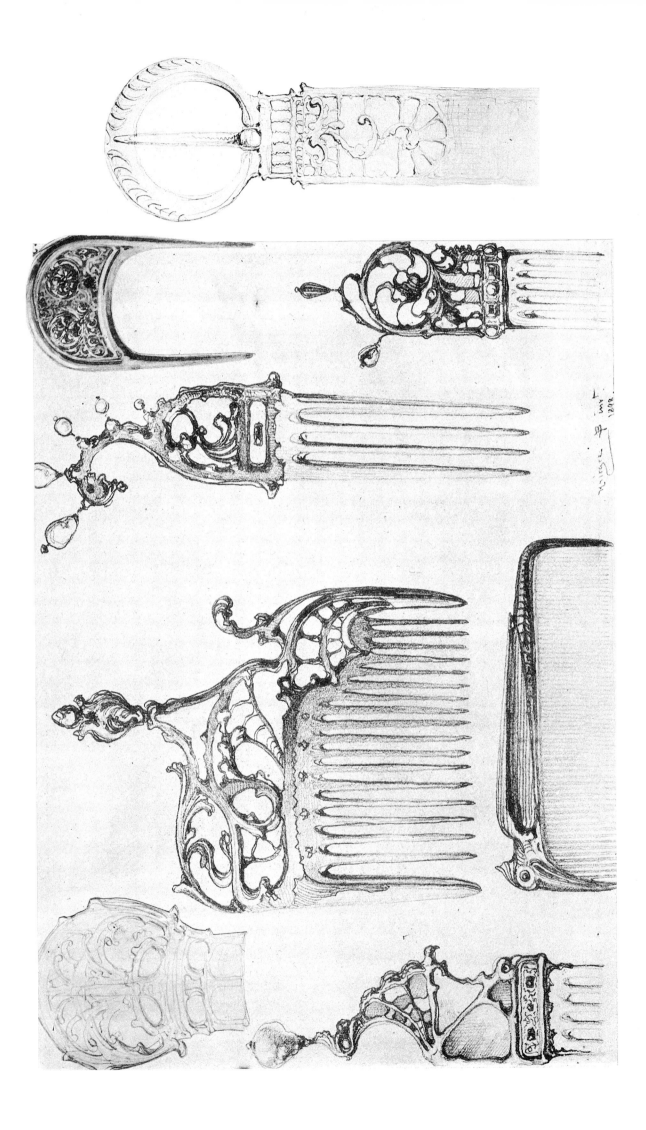

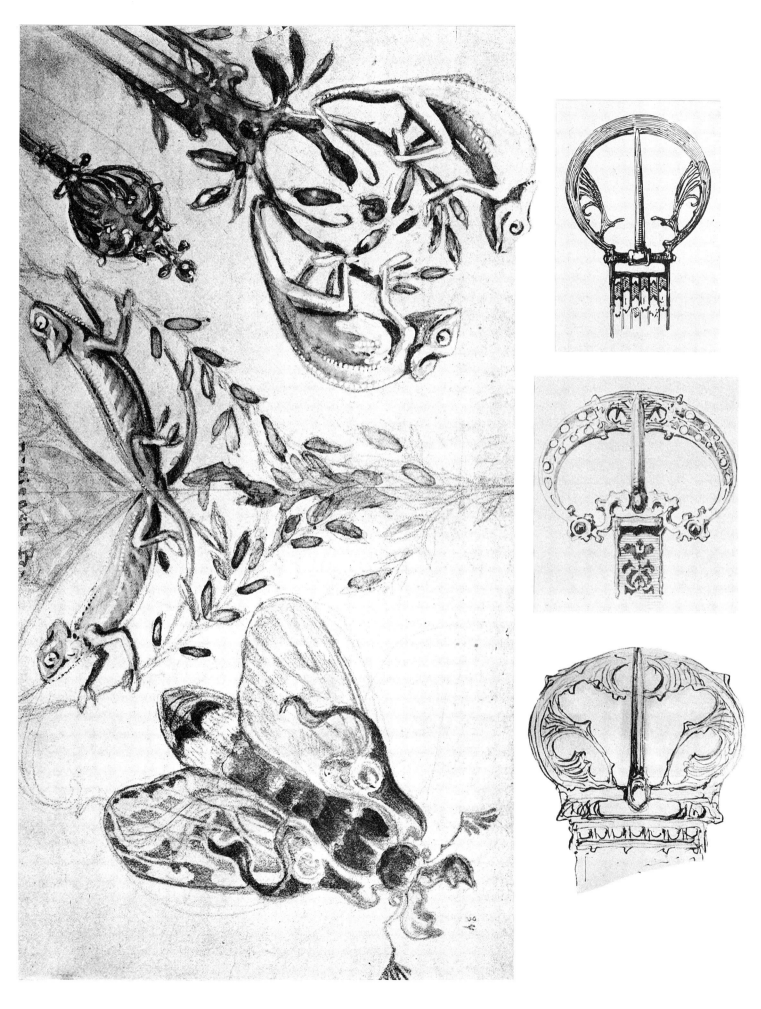

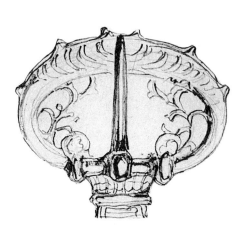

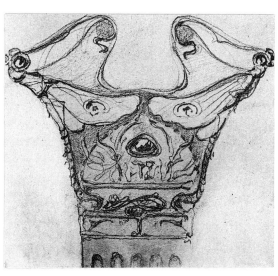

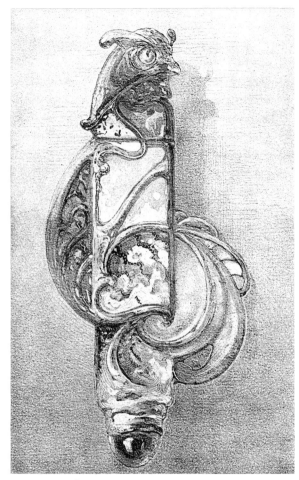

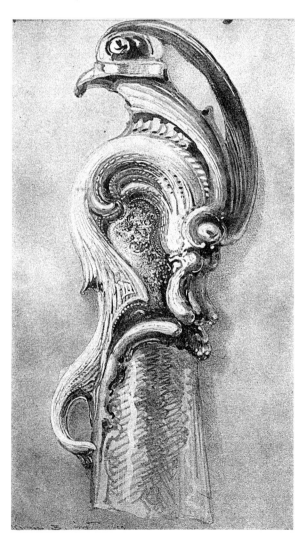

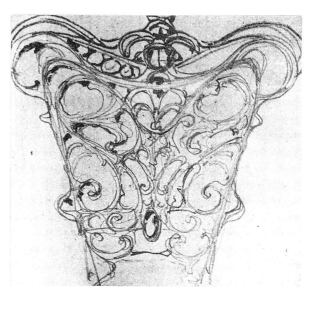

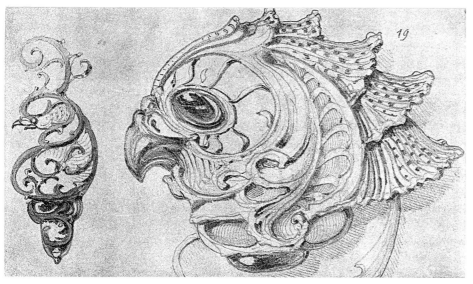

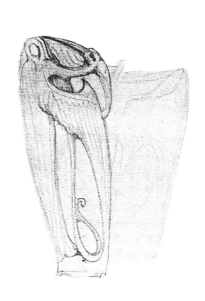

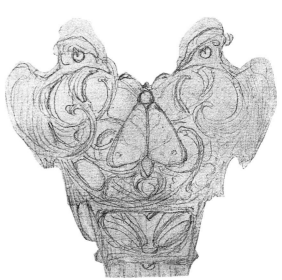

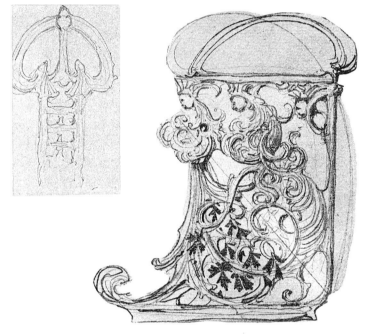

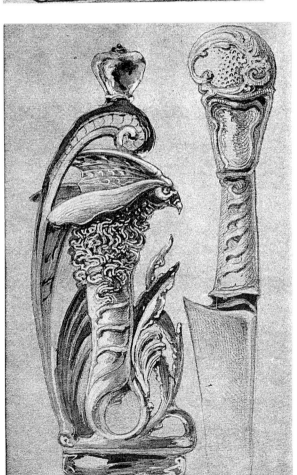

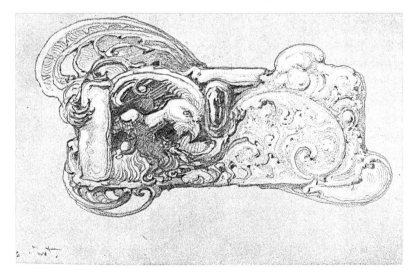

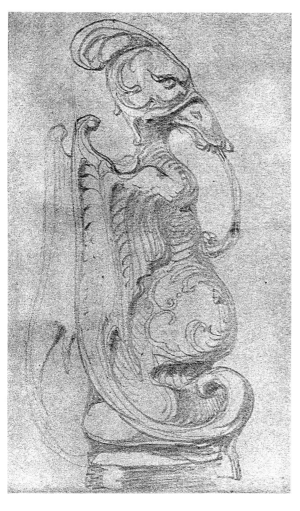

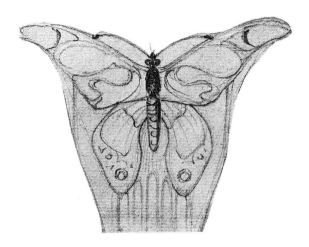

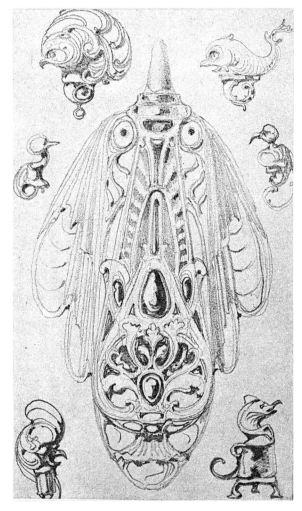

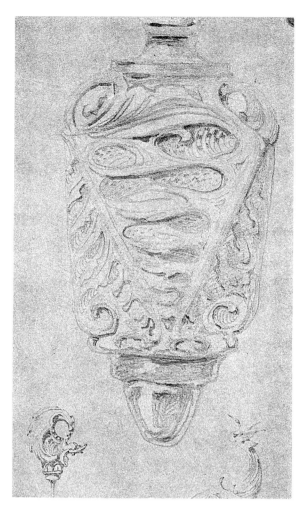

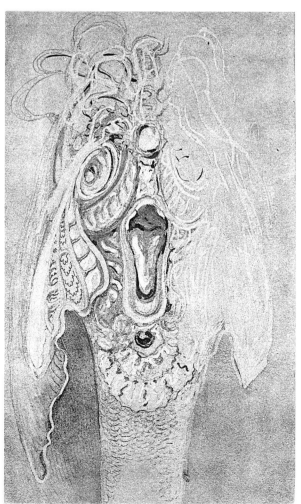

Caméléons

53

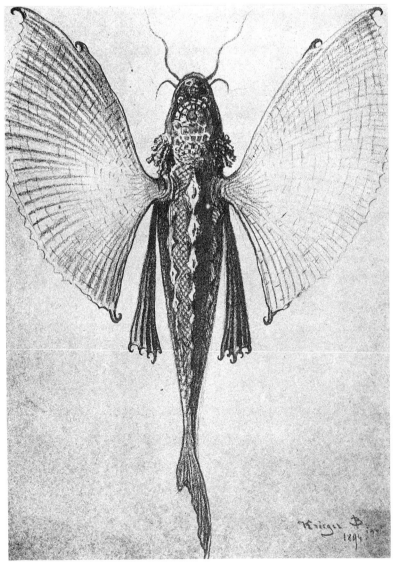

54

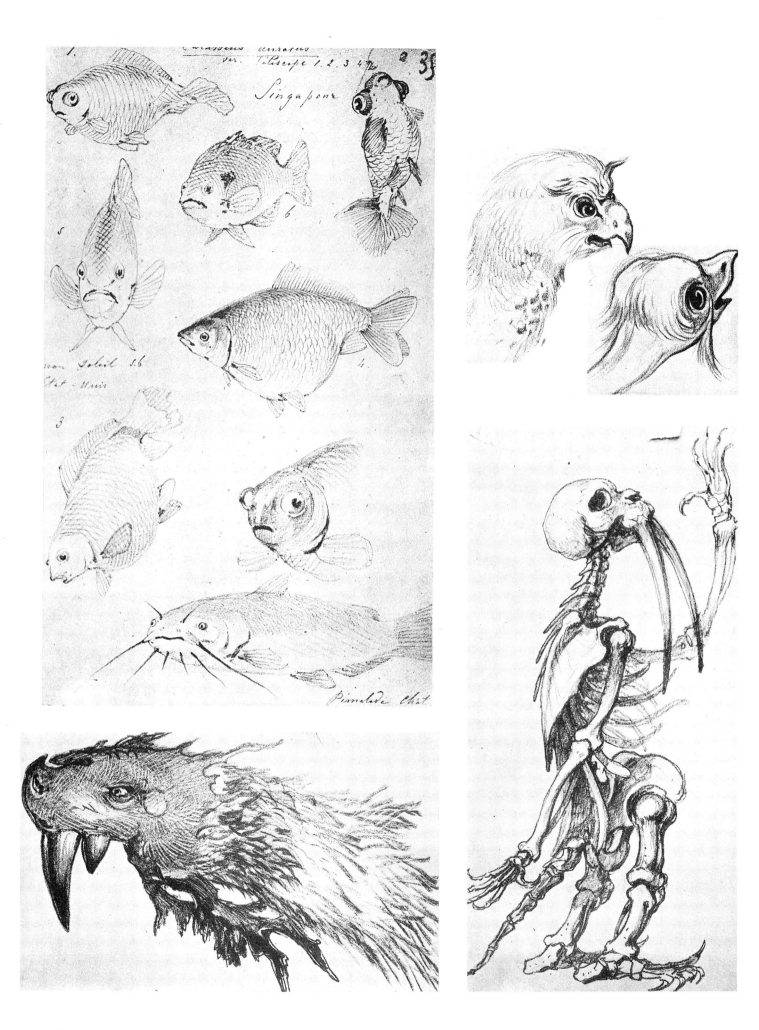

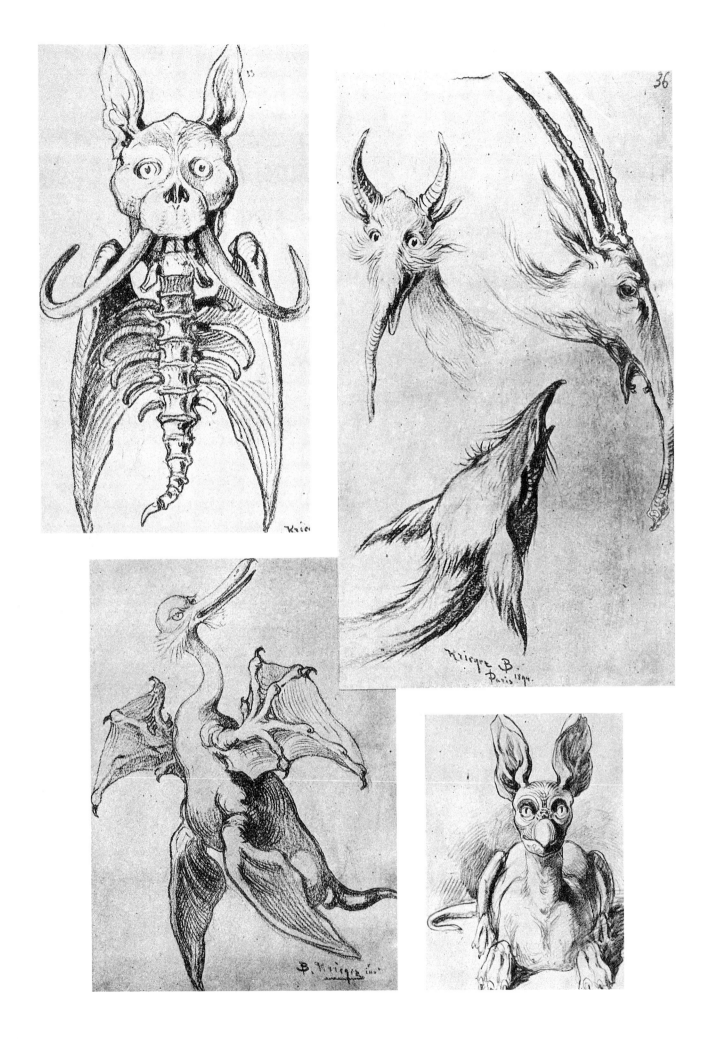

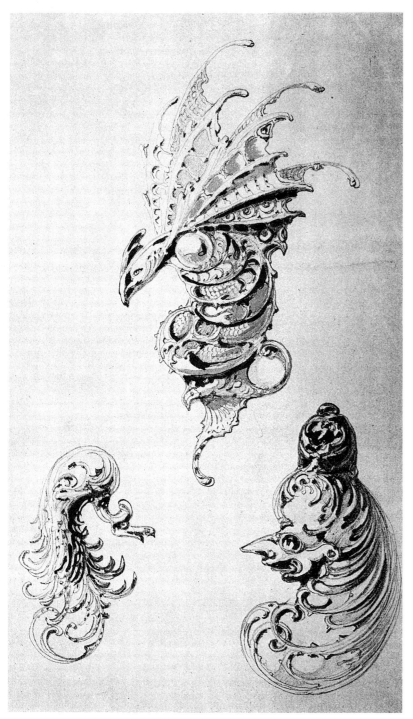

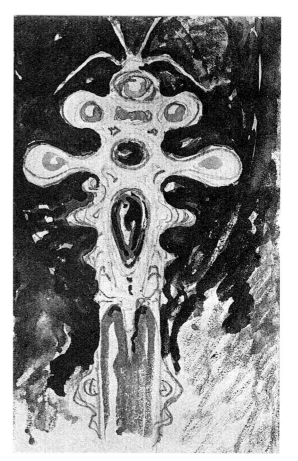

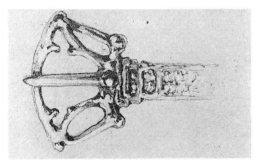

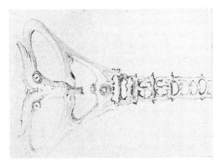

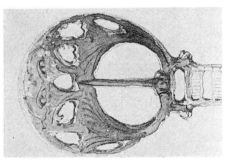

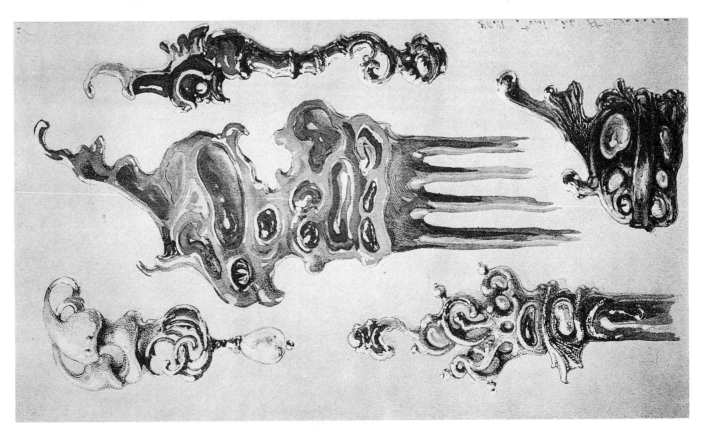

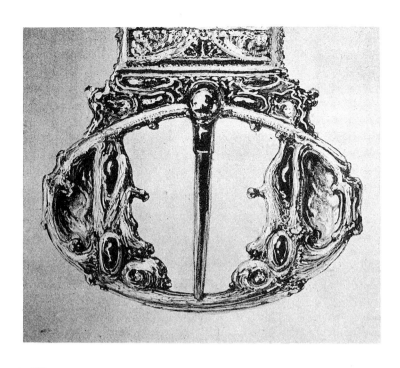

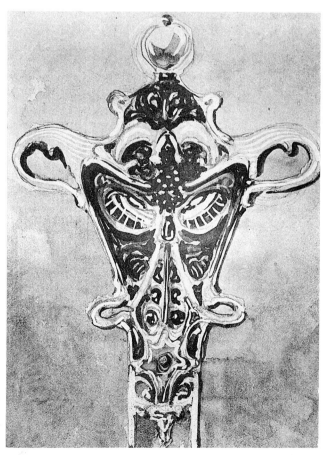

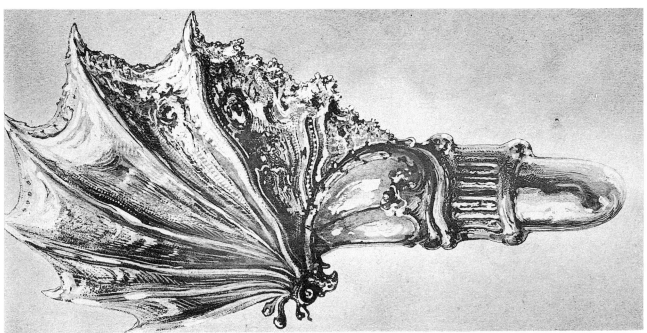

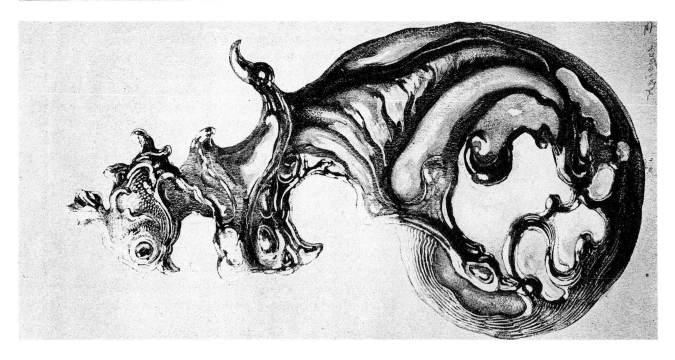

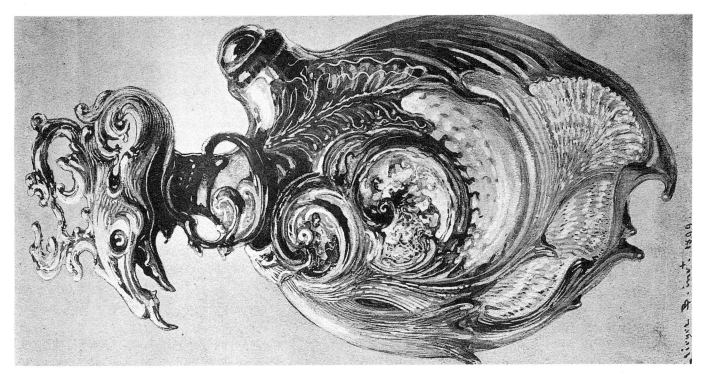

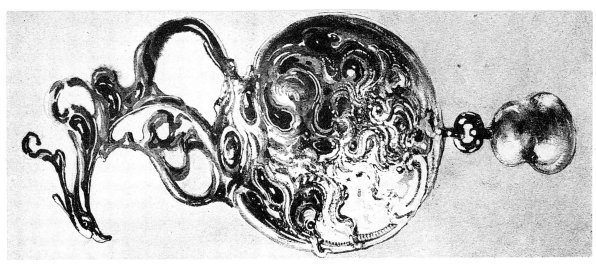

61